GETTING TO KNOW
THE U.S. PRESIDENTS

J A M E S
MADISON

FOURTH PRESIDENT
1809 – 1817

WRITTEN AND ILLUSTRATED BY MIKE VENEZIA

CHILDREN'S PRESS®
A DIVISION OF SCHOLASTIC INC.
NEW YORK   TORONTO   LONDON   AUCKLAND   SYDNEY
MEXICO CITY   NEW DELHI   HONG KONG
DANBURY, CONNECTICUT

Reading Consultant: Nanci R. Vargus, Ed.D., Assistant Professor, School of Education, University of Indianapolis

Historical Consultant: Marc J. Selverstone, Ph.D., Assistant Professor, Miller Center of Public Affairs, University of Virginia

Photographs © 2004:
Architect of the Capitol, Washington, D.C.: 22
Art Resource, NY: 32 (National Portrait Gallery, Smithsonian Institution, Washington, D.C.), 29 (Smithsonian American Art Museum, Washington, D.C.)
Bridgeman Art Library International Ltd., London/New York: 17 (The Crown Estate)
Corbis Images: 3, 26, 30 right, 30 left (Bettmann), 20, 21 (Francis G. Mayer), 10 (Lee Snider), 11, 25
New York Public Library: 7
North Wind Picture Archives: 27, 28
The Mariners' Museum, Newport News, VA: 19
White House Historical Association, White House Collection (123): 5

Colorist for illustrations: Dave Ludwig

Library of Congress Cataloging-in-Publication Data

Venezia, Mike.
  James Madison / written and illustrated by Mike Venezia.
      p. cm. — (Getting to know the U.S. presidents)
Summary: An introduction to the life of James Madison, a man of poor health who could not fight in the Revolutionary War but whose ideas formed the core of the Constitution and Bill of Rights, and who became the nation's fourth president.
  ISBN 0-516-22609-6 (lib. bdg.)   0-516-27478-3 (pbk.)
  1. Madison, James, 1751-1836—Juvenile literature. 2. Presidents—United States—Biography—Juvenile literature. [1. Madison, James, 1751-1836. 2. Presidents.] I. Title. II. Series.
  E342.V46 2003
  973.5'1'092—dc22

                    2003015963

A portrait of
James Madison

James Madison was born in 1751 in the colony of Virginia. He became the fourth president of the United States in 1809. Although James Madison did a pretty good job as president, he is best known for his work in helping to set up the American system of government.

James Madison was one of the nation's smartest presidents. He was also one of the tiniest. As a grown-up, James weighed less than 100 pounds (45 kilograms). A friend once said that James Madison was no bigger than a bar of soap!

A portrait of Dolley Madison
(White House Collection)

Va Va Vooom!
She's Bee-u-tee-ful!
I agree!
Wow!!

I don't understand
what all the
fuss is about.

Me, either.

James' voice was very soft, too. He might have had trouble getting attention if his ideas hadn't been so powerful. People always wanted to hear every word he said.

James also got attention because of his beautiful wife, Dolley. Dolley Madison loved to throw parties. She was very popular and helped her husband's career whenever she could.

James Madison grew up on a large tobacco plantation in Virginia. Virginia was one of thirteen colonies in North America owned and ruled by England.

Today people know that tobacco is bad for your health, but in the 1700s, it was very popular. People would smoke it in pipes, chew it, or, strange as it seems, sniff it up their noses.

Plantation owners made lots of money by selling tobacco to people in the thirteen colonies. They also shipped it across the ocean to sell it to people in England.

An illustration showing Virginia farmland in the 1700s

James Madison was sick a lot when he was a child. He spent much of his time indoors, reading. Fortunately, his father had a large collection of excellent books. When James was feeling good, he enjoyed playing with all the kids who were around. James had brothers and sisters and cousins all over the place.

James also played with the children of his father's slaves. James always believed slavery was very wrong. Still, he couldn't see how large plantations could run without them. Before machines were invented, people were needed to plant and harvest crops. Plantation owners didn't seem to care about their slaves' freedom or rights at all.

Montpelier, shown here as it looks today, was the Madison family home.

When James was about ten years old, his family moved into a large brick mansion a little bit down the road from their first home. His father named the new house Montpelier.

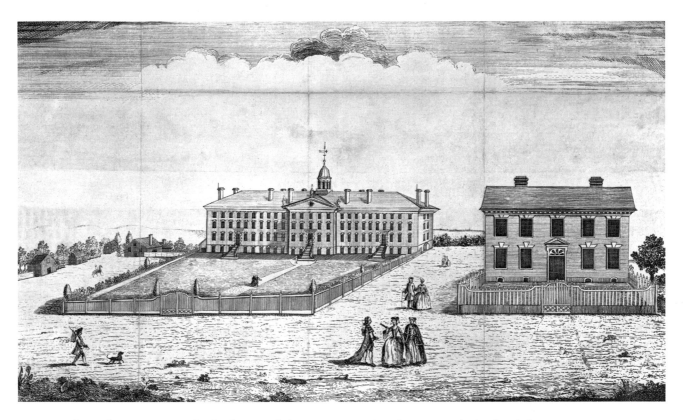

This is how Princeton looked around the time James Madison attended school there.

Soon after the Madisons moved, James was sent to boarding school. He was lucky to have a great teacher there. James learned Latin, Greek, and French, as well as algebra and logic. By the time he was eighteen, James was ready to go to college. James chose the College of New Jersey, which today is called Princeton University.

In colonial times, there were no cars, trains, or planes. Today it would be about a six-hour car ride from James Madison's hometown in Virginia to Princeton, New Jersey. In the 1760s, when people traveled by horse, the same trip could take up to twelve days! When James traveled to Princeton it was the first time he had been out of Virginia.

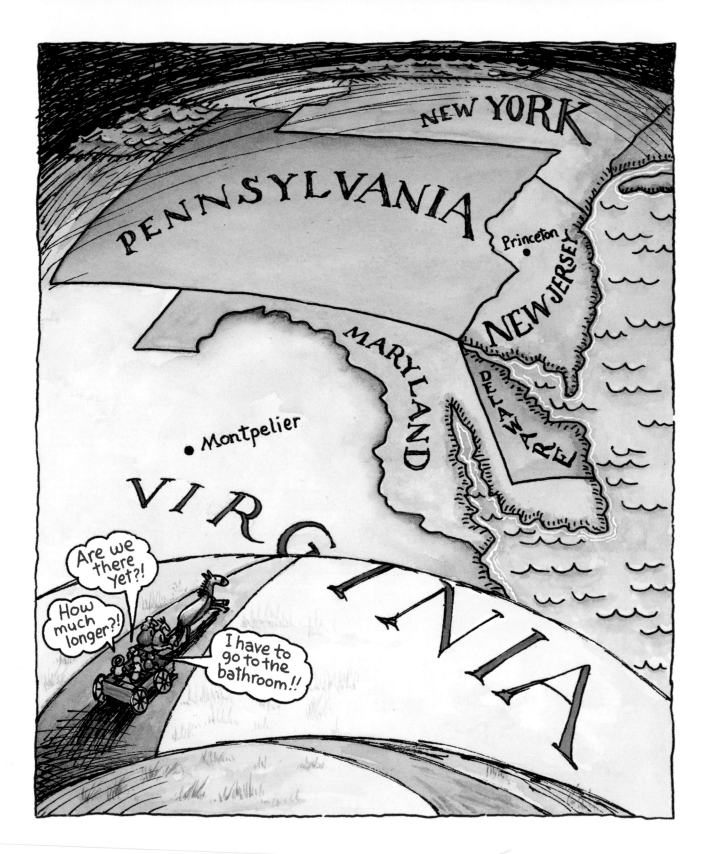

At Princeton, James Madison worked very hard. Students had to get up at 5:00 A.M. and study all day long. James found some time for fun, though. He joined different school clubs and played pranks on his friends.

One of his favorite pranks was to spread greasy feathers in dark doorways and then stand back and watch his classmates slip and slide through the room.

At college, James Madison started to learn about the problems the thirteen colonies were having with England and King George III. Whenever the king needed money for something, he added extra charges, called taxes, to products the colonists needed.

King George III
of England

Students at Princeton were becoming more and more angry about the king's unfair taxes. When James finished college and returned home, he found that the people in Virginia were very angry, too.

Soon James Madison joined in protesting against England's unfair taxes. The English governor of Virginia, Lord Dunmore, decided to pack up and escape to a British warship for his own safety.

A painting showing the shipping port of Norfolk, Virginia

Lord Dunmore wasn't very nice. To get even with the colonists, he sent British soldiers to burn Norfolk, an important shipping port. Now the people of Virginia were furious. They decided to ignore England and set up their own government. James Madison was asked to help do the job.

During this time, the other twelve colonies decided that they wanted independence from England, too. In 1776, leaders of all thirteen colonies got together and signed the Declaration of Independence. With this document, the thirteen colonies declared themselves a brand-new country, the United States of America. Now the war for independence, called the Revolutionary War, got into full swing.

The Death of General Mercer at the Battle of Princeton, January 3, 1777, by John Trumbull

This painting, by John Trumbull, shows the surrender of the British at Yorktown, Virginia, in 1781. (U.S. Capitol Building Rotunda, Washington, D.C.)

Because of his poor health, James never fought in the war. He spent his time helping to create Virginia's government. James came up with lots of good ideas that he would later use to help set up the U.S. government.

After six bloody years of fighting, the Revolutionary War ended. The British surrendered to General George Washington in 1781, and a peace treaty was signed in 1783. The United States of America was officially an independent country!

It seemed like everything should have been fine, but it wasn't. Something was missing. The thirteen new states needed a central government so that they could decide how to do things as one united country. Many states didn't agree with one another. They didn't trust each other very much, either. Something had to be done!

In 1787, each state sent its best men to a convention, or meeting, in Philadelphia to work things out. Virginia's leaders sent James Madison. It was a good thing they did, because James worked harder than almost anyone!

He came up with excellent ideas on how to create a good government. It would be strong enough to control all the states, but be fair to the people who lived in each state. His plan was to have a central government divided into three sections. Each section could keep an eye on the others. This way, no member of the government would become too powerful, as King George had.

This painting, by J. B. Stearns, shows the members of the Constitutional Convention adopting the U.S. Constitution in 1787.

Members of the convention agreed with James' main ideas and used them to put together the United States Constitution. This document explained the rules for the American system of government. But Madison was worried that it didn't say enough about protecting people's rights. He wrote a list of ten basic rights guaranteed to all Americans. This Bill of Rights was soon added to the Constitution.

An illustration showing James Madison (on the right) and Thomas Jefferson working together

Because of his hard work and great ideas, James Madison became known all over the country. He was elected to represent Virginia in the U.S. Congress in 1789. In 1801, when his old friend Thomas Jefferson became president, James was asked to be the nation's secretary of state.

James was in charge of dealing with foreign countries. He soon had to handle a very complicated and dangerous mess. England and France were at war. Whenever they felt like it, they would stop American ships and force sailors to join their side. They also took any cargo they wanted. James and Thomas Jefferson had to work hard to keep the United States from going to war.

British sailors capturing American sailors in the early 1800s

An engraving showing
James Madison as
president

In 1808, James Madison was elected to
be the fourth president of the United States.
England and France were still picking on
American ships.

A painting by Thomas Chambers showing an American ship battling a British ship during the War of 1812 (Smithsonian American Art Museum, Washington, D.C.)

The last thing President Madison wanted was to go to war. But by 1812, he felt forced into it. President Madison had cleverly made a deal with France to leave American ships alone. When the War of 1812 started, it was a fight between the United States and England.

When the British burned Washington, D.C. (left), Dolley Madison grabbed important government papers before fleeing the White House (above).

It was a long war. Most of the time, the United States was getting beaten up pretty badly. British soldiers even marched into Washington, D.C., and burned down lots of buildings.

Dolley Madison barely made it out of the White House alive. She grabbed some valuable historical items and left a hot dinner on the table. Before British soldiers burned the White House, they helped themselves to Dolley and James' dinner!

The American army and navy kept fighting as hard as they could and the war finally ended in 1815.

A portrait by Chester Harding of James Madison as an older man (National Portrait Gallery, Smithsonian Institution, Washington, D.C.)

Soon after the war was over, James Madison's second term as president ended. He returned to his home in Virginia. James spent his time offering advice to his friends in the government. He and Dolley enjoyed entertaining guests, too.

Although James Madison's health was often poor, he lived to the old age of eighty-five. James Madison, known as the Father of the Constitution, died peacefully at Montpelier in 1836.